12 walks around Perthshire

EXPERIENCE BIG T

Felicity Martin

Catkin Press

INTRODUCTION

This guide is the fourth in a series designed to bring together the best walks around Perthshire. It contains 12 routes of varying grades, from 2 to 12 miles in length.

The walks range from gentle strolls to hill climbs. In between are moderate walks that explore forests, river gorges, and loch shores. They have been chosen for their rich wildlife, intriguing history and spectacular views.

Big Tree Country – in all its fascinating aspects – is the common theme. The routes explore bluebell woods, pine forests and veteran trees, and also visit places immortalised by poets and fought over by Picts.

As well as clear directions, each walk includes information to help readers connect with the natural world. Use your senses to experience the wonders of Big Tree Country first hand, by seeing impressive waterfalls, hearing deer bounding through the woods or smelling the honeyed scent of blooming heather.

A car is not needed to make use of the guide, as most of the start points are well served by public transport. The majority of walks can easily be reached by bus and some are also near railway stations. Or why not use a bike to do even more for your fitness and carbon footprint?

COVER: *The Falls of Bruar (Walk 11)*

TITLE PAGES: *Loch of the Lowes, as the sun clears a freezing autumn mist (Walk 5)*

ABOVE: *Autumn colours at Dunkeld on the banks of the River Tay (Walk 5)*

Walking in Perthshire

As Perthshire spans both Lowlands and Highlands, it encompasses flat farmland, rolling hills, high mountains and everything in between. Hundreds of miles of paths thread through these diverse landscapes, offering a wonderful choice of routes.

It is a great place to explore on foot, especially as widespread tree cover means that it is different in every season. In spring, the woods are carpeted in yellow, white and mauve wild flowers. By summer, everything is green with luxuriant foliage. Autumn sets the woods ablaze with red, yellow and gold leaves, while winter frosts turn twigs into a filigree of crystal.

These twelve walks feature many aspects of water in the landscape – especially waterfalls, which are characteristic of Highland Perthshire. **Walk 11: Falls of Bruar & Creag Urrard** begins at the waterfalls made famous by a poem Robert Burns wrote in 1787. The Falls of Acharn on Walk **10: Aberfeldy to Acharn & Kenmore** are less well known, but possibly even more dramatic as they are hidden from view until the last minute.

The shortest route, **Walk 1: Kinloch Rannoch circuit**, has a superb view down wild Loch Rannoch to the Glencoe mountains. A different sort of watery spectacle can be enjoyed on **Walk 2: Rumbling Bridge & River Devon**, where a meandering river suddenly thunders through a deep gorge.

Walk 4: The Knockie & Ardblair starts along the River Ericht in Blairgowrie, following part of The Cateran Trail, Scotland's first circular long distance walk. And **Walk 6: Laggan Hill & Baird's Monument** climbs to a hilltop obelisk before following the peaceful River Earn. The Ericht and the Earn, tributaries of the Tay, are great rivers for salmon and trout.

Most of Scotland's iconic species of wildlife are found in Perthshire's various habitats. The woodland in **Walk 9: Allean Forest & Stones** is home to a whole host of creatures, including red squirrels, pine martens, siskins, crossbills and Scotch argus butterflies. The mountain landscape of **Walk 12: Ben Vorlich & Stuc a' Chroin** is a very different habitat, where you are more likely to see red grouse, ravens, ptarmigan and red deer, or perhaps even a golden eagle.

Half these walks have shorter options, for those who want to explore the area but cover less distance. All but one are circular routes that return to the starting point. The one linear walk uses public transport between start and finish to make a memorable journey through Highland Perthshire.

ABOVE: *Returning towards Loch Earn on the Ben Vorlich path (Walk 12)*

BELOW: *Bluebells in Craig Wood (Walk 5)*

Experience Big Tree Country

Perthshire's remarkable tree and woodland heritage gives it a special look and provides a superb environment for walking. It is a landscape where grand woods and sparkling lochs are set against a backdrop of rugged hills and fertile straths.

Trees grow particularly well in the local climate and soils – often reaching record-breaking proportions. Native trees, such as oak, alder, birch, and Scots pine thrive here. As do larches, spruces, firs and other introduced exotic species, which Perthshire landowners planted extensively in the 18th and 19th centuries to enhance their estates.

Walk 5: Dunkeld Trees & Lochs explores the heart of Big Tree Country. The route starts along the banks of the River Tay, where superb examples of European larch, Wellingtonia, Noble fir, and Douglas fir soar above the path. Later, it visits larch woods, mature beeches, lochside willows and an oakwood carpeted in bluebells.

Scone Palace, which is seen across the Tay on **Walk 7: Rivers Tay & Almond**, has a cathedral-like pinetum with aisles of exotic conifers. Many of these species were discovered in the Americas by the famous plant hunter David Douglas, who began his working life as an apprentice gardener in the palace gardens.

Another impressive collection is Diana's Grove at Blair Castle, the ancestral home of the great tree planters, the Dukes of Atholl. They were the first to grow larches on a large scale for timber, planting millions around Dunkeld and their castle at Blair Atholl. **Walk 11: Bruar & Creag Urrard** goes through Baluain Wood where, to this day, Atholl Estates manage plantations of tall, straight-stemmed larches.

Increasing biodiversity is a priority in many Perthshire woods. At **Walk 8: Moncreiffe Hill & Forts**, the Woodland Trust is doing work to make the wood more varied and open, to create better habitat for birds, butterflies and other creatures.

Fortunately, good management benefits both trees and wildlife, as seen on **Walk 3: Faskally Wood & Lochs**, which visits a model forest. Here open woodland, with a wide mix of mature conifers, shelters a lily-fringed loch that reflects the changing colours of the trees. In autumn, the brilliant spectacle changes after dark, as the Enchanted Forest light and sound show transforms the wood into a magical place.

The **Perthshire Big Tree Country Heritage and Access Project** was set up to care for and celebrate this special environment. The project has improved access and interpretation at over 20 woodland sites throughout Perthshire. On these walks, you will use paths and see interpretation boards, wood and rock carvings resulting from this work, and also pass through woodlands now sensitively maintained and improved.

Perthshire Big Tree Country is at the centre of the ICONIC project, a global rescue operation to save some of the world's most threatened conifer species. Collections of different conifer species from all over the temperate world are being established in Perthshire forests, estates and gardens, where their performance will be closely monitored to aid ongoing research.

Several organisations are partners in Perthshire Big Tree Country, an initiative led by Perth and Kinross Countryside Trust (PKCT). Other project work by PKCT and its partners includes preserving and interpreting Perthshire Redwoods and the historic orchards of the Carse of Gowrie.

Perth and Kinross Countryside Trust was established in 1997 and aims to provide and promote high quality opportunities for outdoor access and recreation throughout Perth and Kinross.

PKCT

Contact details:
01738 475255
www.pkct.org
www.perthshirebigtreecountry.co.uk

LEFT: *The Parent Larch on the Big Tree Trail (Walk 5)*

ABOVE: *Giant Sequoias (Wellingtonias) in Scone Palace pinetum*

1

The conical peak of Schiehallion, the 'fairy mountain', is a prominent landmark on this short walk set in a magnificent wild landscape with waterfall, river and loch.

Kinloch Rannoch circuit

Start	Kinloch Rannoch – The Square **NN661587**
Grade	■□□□□
Distance	1.6 or 3.2km (1 or 2 miles)
Ascent	50m (165ft)
Time	0.5 to 1.5 hours
Terrain	Riverside, wooded hillside and loch shore, linked by paths and short sections of road.

Getting there: Kinloch Rannoch is 20 miles west of Pitlochry, via the B8019 and B846. Park in the Square beside the Dunalastair Hotel.

Public transport: Buses from Pitlochry.

This walk consists of two loops that make a figure of eight with the village at its centre. It can be done as one walk, or two individual walks of about a mile each, both starting from the Square, where a large monument to the Gaelic poet Dugald Buchanan stands.

1 NN661587 From the Square, walk to the right of the church and along the road in the Pitlochry direction. Turn right down Allt Mor Crescent. Just before the Primary School, go right on a path down the near side of the Allt Mor, a lively burn.

2 NN663587 Cross a footbridge over the burn and walk between the school and the fast-flowing River Tummel. Where the tarmac path swings left between the houses, keep straight ahead on a grassy path through birch woodland. Follow it through a car park, with a view to Schiehallion. About 50m beyond, go up a few steps to the main road.

3 NN670587 Cross with care and go through a metal gate on the opposite side. Walk ahead for 50m then go left onto an old trackway that slopes uphill through deciduous woodland. It soon levels off and runs parallel to the road, below the crags of Craig Varr. Oak trees predominate until you go through a gate with a stile beside it, into birch woodland with coppiced hazel below the track.

4 NN665588 About 200m beyond the gate, fork left onto a path marked by a yellow arrow and go through a swing gate. The path runs between the wood and road to Kinloch Rannoch Outdoor Centre, where you continue across the road bridge over the Allt Mor. *If you want to omit the second loop, follow the road back to the Square.*

5 NN662588 After crossing the road bridge, pass one cottage then turn right up a track to an information board, where there is a view of the Allt Mor waterfall. Go through a wooden gate into

the wood. Fork left off the stony track after 20m onto a grassy path that runs along the bottom edge of the wood, with views over the village. The path is rough and wet in places, especially near a covered well.

6 NN656588 The path narrows and dips down to a kissing gate onto the main road by Loch Rannoch holiday lodges. Turn left along the road, walking above the shore of Loch Rannoch. You can access the shore from a lay-by where the road bends left. Continue on the road towards the village.

7 NN659586 After passing the first stone cottage, turn right then go through the gate on your left onto a track. Pass an electricity substation and bear left through another gate to a grassy area beside the dam that controls the flow of water out of Loch Rannoch.

8 NN660584 Continue on the path, which follows the river downstream through birch and aspen woodland. Immediately after passing under the arched stone road bridge, go left up a path with dilapidated steps. Walk around a disused toilet block and back up to the Square.

OPPOSITE: *Allt Mor waterfall in winter (Point 5)*

ABOVE: *The Square in Kinloch Rannoch (Point 1)*

BELOW: *Schiehallion seen across the River Tummel from the car park (near Point 3)*

Kinloch Rannoch, a quiet village in the far northwest of Perthshire, is situated where the River Tummel flows out of Loch Rannoch. Although the area seems remote these days, it lay on the old 'Road to the Isles', one of the major routes for cattle drovers and other travellers between central Scotland and the Hebridean islands. Plaques on several cairns placed in parking spots from Garry Bridge to Rannoch Station illustrate the history of this route. The modern tarmac road ends at Rannoch Station, 18 miles west of the village. Beyond lies the vast wilderness of Rannoch Moor where long walking routes lead to Glencoe and Fort William.

Loch Rannoch's shores are steeped in legend. If you drive or cycle around the loch, look out for the Clan Trail – information boards relating tales of the local clans. The Black Wood of Rannoch lies on the south side; this remnant of the ancient Caledonian Forest contains many old, gnarled Scots pines.

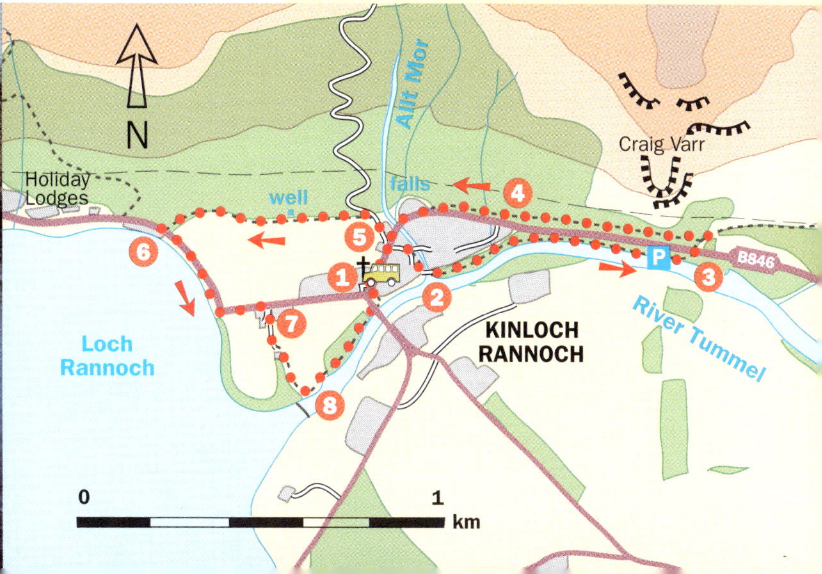

2

On this gentle stroll by the River Devon, the soundscape changes from a soothing babble to a roaring cascade, as the river flows through pastures then into a dramatic gorge.

Rumbling Bridge & River Devon

Start	Crook of Devon – main street (A977) **NO034002**
Grade	■□□□□
Distance	5.6km (3.5 miles)
Ascent	40m (130ft)
Time	2 hours
Terrain	Riverside paths and woodland tracks, fairly level except around the gorge.

Getting there: Leave the M90 at Kinross and take the A977 west for 4 miles to Crook of Devon.

Public transport: Bus service from Kinross and Stirling.

Rumbling Bridge spans a deep gorge where water racing through narrow rock walls creates a thunderous roar. Here the River Devon, which flows out of the Ochils, tumbles through an eroded gap in hard strata of volcanic agglomerate. One particularly noisy feature is the Devil's Mill, so called because the churning water continues to grind rocks on a Sunday. The permanently high humidity enables lush vegetation of ferns, mosses and liverworts to grow in the gorge. The original Rumbling Bridge, built in 1713, had steep approaches on either side and no parapets. In 1816 another bridge was built over it, 120 feet above the water.

PERTHSHIRE BIG TREE COUNTRY

The Kinross-shire village of Crook of Devon is where the River Devon takes a sharp bend, diverted by a bed of hard rocks that it eventually breaks through at Rumbling Bridge. This route follows the river then loops around Lendrick Muir, a large neo-classical mansion that was a school from 1946 to 1998 and is now a Christian activity centre used by groups of children and young people.

The going is easy, except around Rumbling Bridge gorge, where the path is narrower with several flights of steps down to viewpoints. This section can be omitted by crossing the footbridge from **3** to **5**.

Parking places are limited on the main street in Crook of Devon. An alternative start point for this circuit is by the bridge in Rumbling Bridge (**4**), where there is a large lay-by and a bus stop.

ABOVE: *Rumbling Bridge gorge from one of the viewpoints (between Points 4 and 5)*

RIGHT: *Relaxing by the bend in the River Devon (just before Point 3)*

1 NO034002 Starting from Fossoway Stores and The Inn at the centre of Crook of Devon, head westwards along the A977, in the Rumbling Bridge direction. Walk along the pavement on the right side of the road, soon passing the junction with Naemoor Road (the return route).

2 NT029998 Keep going for 140m beyond the end of speed limit sign, then turn right down steps onto a path beside the River Devon. Some fine trees grow on the grassy banks, including big beeches with silvery trunks. About 1km downstream, both river and path bend left towards Rumbling Bridge gorge.

3 NT018999 Just beyond the bend, pass the upper footbridge *(a possible shortcut)* then a stone-walled viewpoint. Continue on the near side of the river, ignoring a path to the right, which goes down steps to the middle bridge. Keep on through woodland to a kissing gate, where you turn right onto a road.

4 NT016995 Cross the road bridge, high above the river, and immediately turn right through a metal gate, where there is a big step down. Follow the path beside the gorge; a railing protects you from the drop where it runs near the edge. Three viewpoints are worth visiting along the way, all with steps down into the gorge: the first gives a view of the unusual double road bridge, the next is a platform built out over the water, the third is at Devil's Mill, where the water squeezes through a narrow gap then churns into a boiling pot. Continue all the way up this side, ignoring a right turn to 'Upper Gorge', a path across the middle bridge.

5 NT018999 Pass the upper bridge again and go through a swing gate onto a minor road. Turn right along the road for 200m then go left by a public path sign onto a tarmac drive. The Ochil Hills rise ahead and Lendrick Muir is on the right. Pass a conifer wood with a track into Lendrick Muir and continue past the next field.

6 NO017006 At the next strip of woodland, turn right through a pedestrian gate and walk along a track on the edge of the trees. Beyond the field, the track enters woodland. At a fork, go left and walk through the mixed age conifers for 800m, ignoring side turnings. Where the track ends, continue to the left on a path through an open area under power lines.

7 NO027009 Go through a kissing gate and down onto the river bank. Walk to the right, through another gate and along a water meadow, following the river downstream with an open view across it. Follow the path to the right through a swing gate and uphill away from the river. Walk between the fenced fields of a deer farm to Naemoor Road. Turn left and cross the River Devon again by an arched stone bridge to a T-junction with the A977. Turn left back to the start.

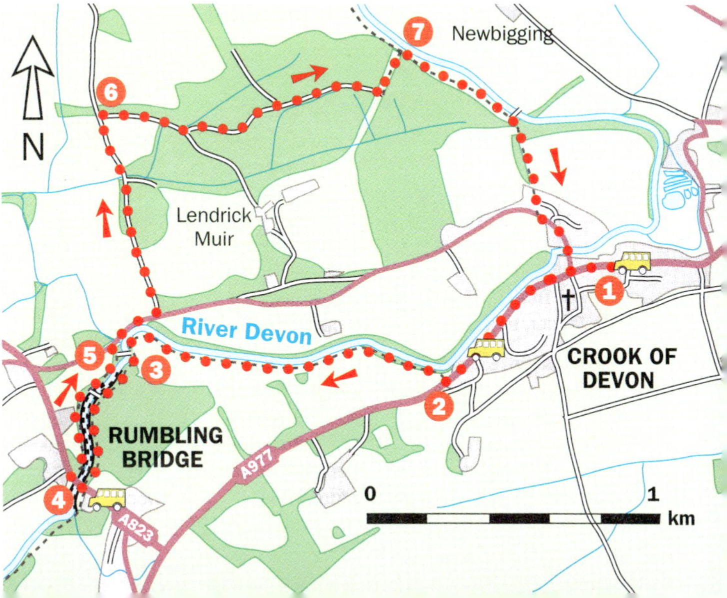

3

Tall trees shelter tranquil Loch Dunmore, in contrast to larger Loch Faskally where open views stretch over birch-covered hillsides to rugged mountains.

Faskally Wood & Lochs

Start Pitlochry – Rie-Achan car park **NN936582**

Grade ■□□□□

Distance 6.4km (4 miles)

Ascent 90m (300ft)

Time 2 hours

Terrain Paths by wooded loch shores; easy walking except for several flights of steps.

Getting there: From the A9 follow the A924 (Atholl Road) and turn down Rie-Achan Road at the north end of town to the public car park (pay and display).

Public transport: The start is adjacent to the bus station and 250m west of the railway station.

Faskally Wood was created as a 'model forest' in the 19th century and in the 1950s became a training ground for young foresters who learnt how to manage woodland diversity. At its heart lies picturesque Loch Dunmore, which has an all abilities path around it. The loch's still waters mirror spring and autumn foliage beautifully, and water lilies bloom in July and August. It is the site of the Enchanted Forest light and sound show each autumn (www.enchantedforest.org.uk).

PERTHSHIRE BIG TREE COUNTRY

Pitlochry Dam was built across the River Tummel as part of an extensive hydroelectric scheme. It was opened in 1950 and houses turbines that generate renewable electricity from water power. The dam created a new loch – Loch Faskally – but also imposed an obstacle to salmon migrating up-river to spawn. This problem was solved by building a fish ladder, enabling them to bypass the dam.

The Explorers Garden is at Pitlochry Festival Theatre, just downstream from Pitlochry Dam. It showcases flower and tree species discovered around the world by Scottish plant hunters. Many of the tree species are now grown for timber in Perthshire forests.

This is an easy route apart from steps up and down the loch shore. Alternative start points are at the (free) car parks by Pitlochry Dam and in Faskally Wood.

1 **NN936582** Walk down Rie-Achan Road, and under a railway bridge. Turn left up Armoury Road and follow it as it bends right, downhill towards Pitlochry Dam. Cross the walkway over the dam, pausing for the view up Loch Faskally and down the River Tummel. On the far side, have a look at the fish ladder, before going right on a narrow path along the wooded loch shore. A bench is sited with a fine view across the loch to Ben Vrackie.

2 **NN932576** Cross a wooden footbridge over a stream and climb a long flight of steps up the bank. Keep ahead on a wide tarmac path that runs between the noisy A9 road and the loch. Go through a gate by a stone house and turn right onto the minor road to Clunie. After passing under the A9 flyover, turn right, down a path towards the loch.

3 **NN927585** Walk across the arching Clunie footbridge, which gives a bird's-eye view of the loch. Turn left on the far side and pass a viewpoint where an old stone bridge crossed the river before the loch was created. Follow a rough path along the shore. Just beyond a little footbridge, turn right (for Killiecrankie) and zigzag up the slope, climbing a flight of steps. The path bends left into Faskally Wood.

4 NN924588 Fork right at the second of two broad path junctions. Keep on the main path, which runs through tall larch and Douglas fir. Dip downhill to a path junction by Loch Dunmore, where the return route joins from the left (**6**). Take the next left to go around the loch anti-clockwise (ahead leads to the car park). Stay on the path beside the loch, walking under Scots pines and passing the Chinese Bridge, where stone carvings depict some of the local wildlife.

5 NN920592 Keep left at the head of the loch to return down the west shore of Loch Dunmore, passing a boathouse and rounding a bay. Beyond a bench with a view over the water, rise up around a rock outcrop then pass the Chinese Bridge again. Loop around the foot of the loch to the path junction where you started the circuit.

6 NN921589 Turn right uphill to retrace your route to Clunie footbridge. Instead of crossing the bridge, keep ahead and walk under the A9 flyover, construction of which is commemorated by a cairn beside the path. Beyond, the path bends left, downhill to a secluded bay where you'll find Pitlochry Boating Station and café. Turn right here, up a tarmac lane.

7 NN932585 Just before meeting the main road, turn right down Lagreach Brae. Where the road bends left, walk to the right of the houses down a path into woodland.

Follow the path left, along the shore of Loch Faskally, staying on the path nearest the loch. Beyond a small bay, go left across a wide grassy area to the parking area by the dam. Turn left up the lane and back under the railway bridge to the start.

ABOVE TOP: *View across Loch Faskally to Ben Vrackie and the return route along the wooded loch shore (Point 2)*

ABOVE MIDDLE: *The Enchanted Forest lights up Loch Dunmore in Faskally Wood (Point 5)*

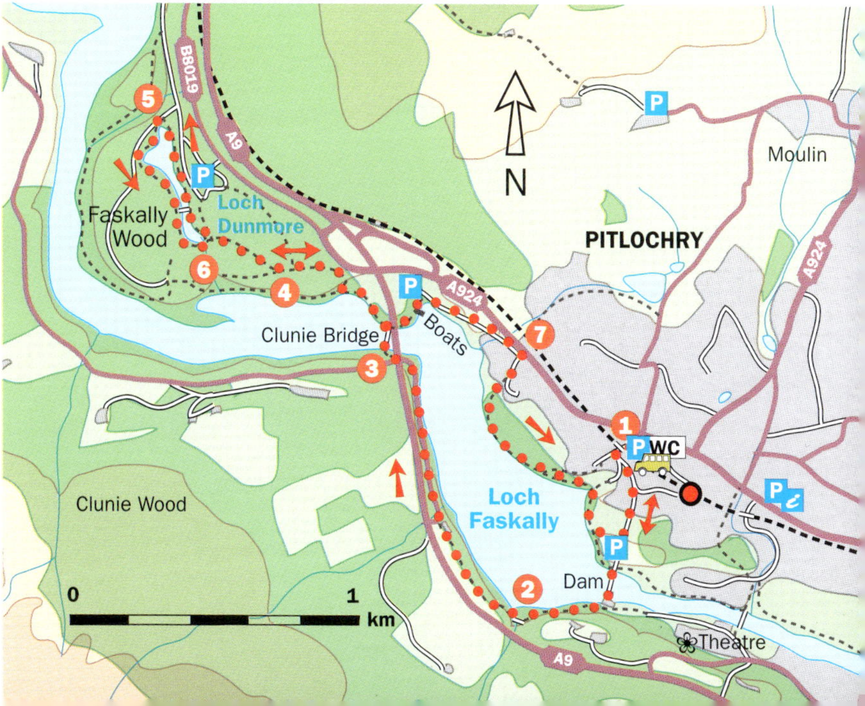

4

This circuit around Blairgowrie begins beside the fast-flowing River Ericht on shady woodland paths that are a contrast to the open spaces and wide views on the hill above.

The Knockie & Ardblair

Start	Blairgowrie – Riverside car park **NO180454**
Grade	■□□□□
Distance	9.6km (6 miles)
Ascent	170m (560ft)
Time	3 hours
Terrain	Paths, farm tracks and roads along a river bank, through farmland and woods, and over a rounded hill with extensive views.

Getting there: Take the A93 from Perth to Blairgowrie and, just before the traffic lights with the A923 (beside the triangular Wellmeadow), turn left along Lower Mill Street, then go right, downhill into Riverside car park.

Public transport: Bus services from Perth, Dunkeld, Coupar Angus, Alyth and Dundee.

Ardblair Wood is mixed woodland of birch and oak, with some mature Scots pine. It is rich in moss, ferns and wild flowers, including the small but prolific pink purslane. As the ground is wet, the path through it is slightly raised. The wood has a disused curling pond on its east edge and is situated close to the old weaving hamlet of Muirton of Ardblair. Nearby Ardblair Castle, home to the Blair Oliphant family, dates back to 1115.

The Knockie is a rounded hill with a marvellous view from the top. It is an outlier of the Grampian Mountains that rise to the northwest of the vale of Strathmore, the fertile plain on which Blairgowrie lies. Its name is derived from 'cnoc', the Gaelic for a small hill.

Blairgowrie is a market town at the heart of the soft fruit growing district of east Perthshire. This walk starts beside the River Ericht, which once powered flax and jute mills employing many workers. It combines the Knockie Path and the Ardblair Trail, two waymarked routes on the Blairgowrie Path Network, and passes ancient woods and castles connected with local clans.

1 NO180454 Facing the river, turn left up the riverside path. Heart symbols mark the Cateran Trail long distance route (www.caterantrail.org). Go up a flight of steps at the end of the grassy area and turn right along a track. In 150m divert right down steps to a river viewpoint with information about salmon migration. Another 50m on, fork right on a path to Cargill's Leap viewpoint above a rocky narrows. Continue on the path to a disused mill by a footbridge that gives a great view over the river. Turn uphill by the mill, back onto the track and go right along it, passing some restored mill buildings.

2 NO171464 The track bends left, beside Lornty Burn to join a tarmac road. Turn left uphill, passing a farm and gaining a view over the valley. At a junction, where there is a bench, turn right along a hard track with a sign for East Gormack. Steadily climb past fields, with a view across Lornty Burn.

3 NO162459 At the crest of the hill, turn left through a pedestrian gate onto a path across a field. Walk over the brow of the Knockie to a bench, an information board about Newton and Ardblair Castles, and a viewpoint indicator with a wide panorama over Strathmore to the Sidlaw Hills. Continue down a track, past Maryfield farm, and bend left into a residential area. Turn right down Newton Street.

4 NO174452 Turn right at the first crossroads into Adams Way, which leads to the Gallowhill path running between fields. This path bends downhill to the A923. Turn right along the pavement for 250m.

5 NO168447 Cross the road and go left to Myreside farm. Follow the track to the right of the farm buildings then through wetlands. At a T-junction by tall pines, go left along the 'Weasel Roadie', which gently rises up to the B947. Cross the road and walk ahead on a track, keeping left at a junction.

OPPOSITE: *Resting at the Knockie viewpoint (after Point 3)*

6 NO171437 Turn left through a gate into Ardblair Wood and follow the path through it. Exit by a kissing gate and cross a field to the A93. Go left for 40m then right by green railings onto a path through a residential area. Keep straight ahead, crossing a road, to a T-junction. Following signs on lamp posts, turn left, then left again into Cedar Avenue and right into Paterson Drive. At the next junction, go left into Holly Crescent and, where it bends right, keep ahead on a path to the A923.

7 NO182445 Walk to the left then, by a mini roundabout, turn right along Blairgowrie House Road. Pass an old farm steading and join a stony path going downhill. Walk around sharp bends to a minor road in an industrial area. Turn left, passing supermarkets, to the centre. Go around the Wellmeadow (right then left) and turn right along Lower Mill Street back to the car park.

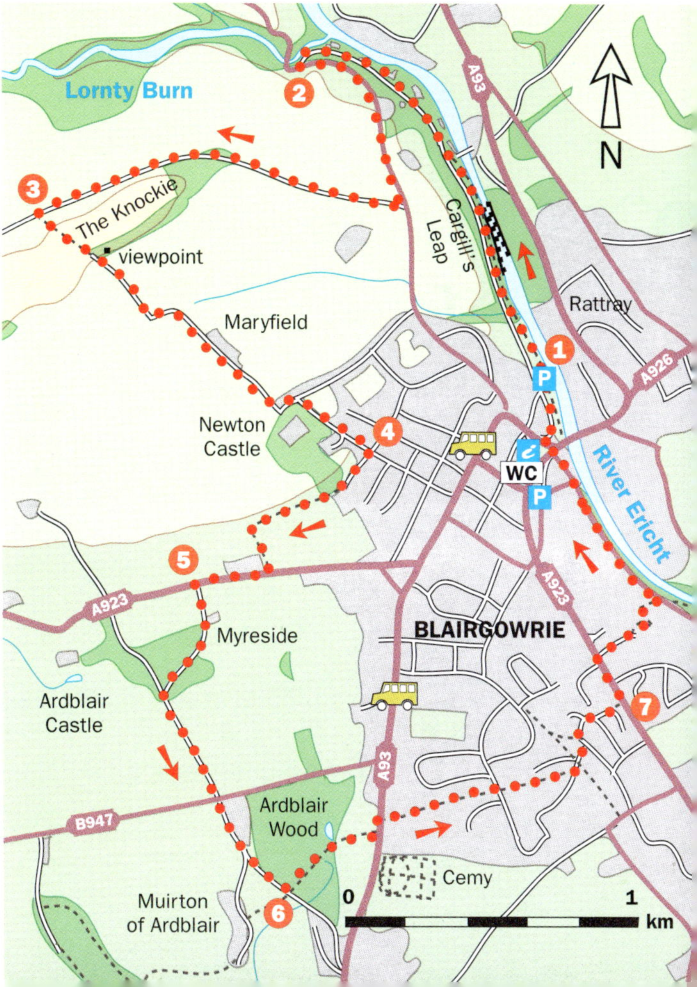

5

Dunkeld's woods abound with heritage trees, red squirrels and fallow deer, whilst the lochs and river are home to otter, osprey and wildfowl.

Dunkeld Trees & Lochs

Start Dunkeld – Atholl Street (North) car park **NO026428**

Grade ■■□□□

Distance 11.2km (7 miles)

Ascent 150m (500ft)

Time 3.5 hours

Terrain River bank, grassy fields and varied woodland with a network of paths and tracks.

Getting there: Leave the A9 15 miles north of Perth and take the A923 through Dunkeld to the car park.

Public transport: Buses to Dunkeld from Perth, Aberfeldy, Blairgowrie and Pitlochry; trains to Dunkeld & Birnam station, on south side of the River Tay.

ABOVE: *Loch of the Lowes and Scottish Wildlife Trust hide on an autumn morning (Point 8)*

Hilton Dunkeld House Hotel is set in a 280-acre estate where the Dukes of Atholl once had their summer home. During the 18th and 19th centuries the Dukes planted numerous trees in their grounds, introducing species, such as the larch, that were new to Scotland. The Parent Larch, which dates from 1738, was the source of seed from which millions of trees were grown. Significant trees are numbered as part of a Big Tree Trail, through the hotel grounds.

Loch of the Lowes is one of a string of lochs between Dunkeld and Blairgowrie. It is a wildlife reserve where the main attraction, from early April to late August, is a pair of breeding ospreys. The loch and its surrounds are rich in wildlife. In early winter, 3,000 greylag geese roost on the loch, while other birds, such as great spotted woodpeckers, can be seen all year. Fallow and roe deer, red squirrels and pine martens are also regularly seen from the Scottish Wildlife Trust visitor centre, which is open from 10am to 5pm all year round.

Craig Wood is a mature oakwood that is carpeted with bluebells in the spring.

Dunkeld is a historic small town that became an ecclesiastical centre in 820AD. The walk starts past Dunkeld Cathedral, which dates from 1325. It was ruined during the Reformation and has since been partially restored to serve as the parish church. It is open on weekdays and Sunday afternoons. The Little Houses in Cathedral Street date from the 18th century, when the town was rebuilt after being burnt down during the Jacobite rebellion. The route uses paths that are part of the Dunkeld Walks Network.

1 **NO026428** From the car park, walk past Stanley Hill – a wooded mound – and turn left. Follow a path that skirts Dunkeld Cathedral. *Alternatively, go left across the grass and through an archway to the square where the Visitor Information Centre is located. Then go right up Cathedral Street into the Cathedral grounds (when open) and rejoin the path by a gate on the right.*

2 **NO023426** Beyond Dunkeld Cathedral, go left into woodland, meeting the Big Tree Trail between the Parent Larch (17) and the UK's champion Douglas fir (18). Keep left through the trees, then go right along the main path beside the River Tay, enjoying lovely views over the water. After 1km, join the Dunkeld House Hotel drive by a National Cycle Network sign. Head towards the hotel and fork right in front of it.

3 **NO010426** Keep right behind the hotel and walk up the rear drive, passing holiday lodges. The drive leads uphill, through woodland full of quad bike tracks, to a road. Cross over to Polney Loch, which reflects the steep, wooded slopes of Craig a' Barns.

4 **NO014430** Walk 40m to the right and join a path along the south shore of the loch. At the east end, go straight ahead onto a track that gradually climbs through larch woodland. Stay on the main way, passing above sawmills.

5 **NO023437** Walk through Cally car park to a crossroads of tracks. Go straight over into open woodland. On a bend, turn right and immediately right again to go downhill on a grassy track. About 30m beyond a gateway, fork left onto a path through a beech wood above the A923. Where it meets the road, cross over and go a few paces right to a junction.

6 **NO030432** Turn left up the Dunkeld & Birnam Golf Club drive. Keep right as you cross the car park, then go down a path and left to a kissing gate. Walk across fields with a view of the pretty hamlet of Fungarth. Join a lane and turn right along it. After passing a white-washed house, continue on a grassy track that dips down across a wet area.

7 **NO041429** Meet a path above and go left along it for 300m. Beyond a gate, turn left downhill to a road. Cross over and go left on a path along the wooded shore of Loch of the Lowes to the visitor centre.

8 **NO040435** Retrace your outward route to **7** then keep ahead on the upper path. Beyond a kissing gate, turn right down a broad track. Follow it steeply downhill, keeping right to skirt the lower edge of Craig Wood.

9 **NO033424** Meet a road and turn right, towards Dunkeld. The view stretches over the town as you descend Brae Street. At a crossroads, turn right along the main shopping street to the car park.

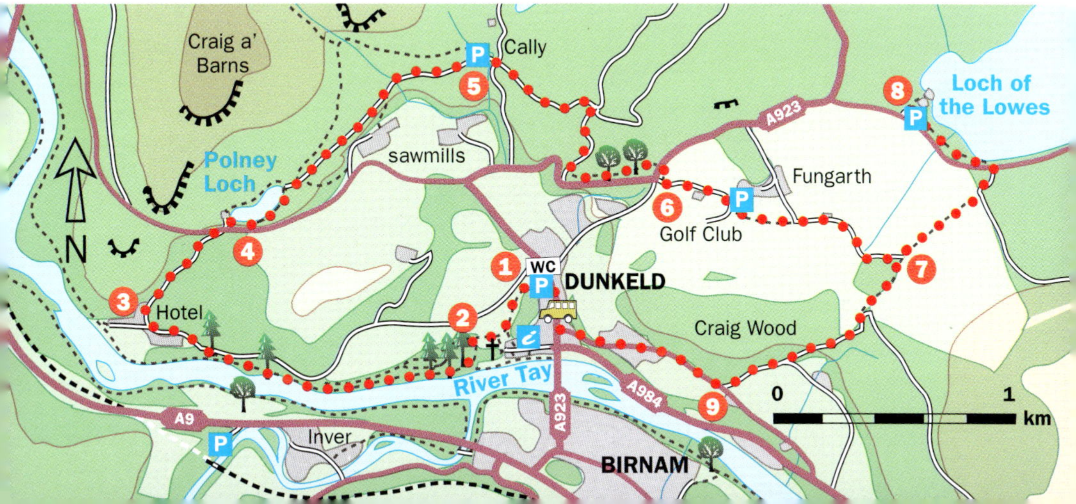

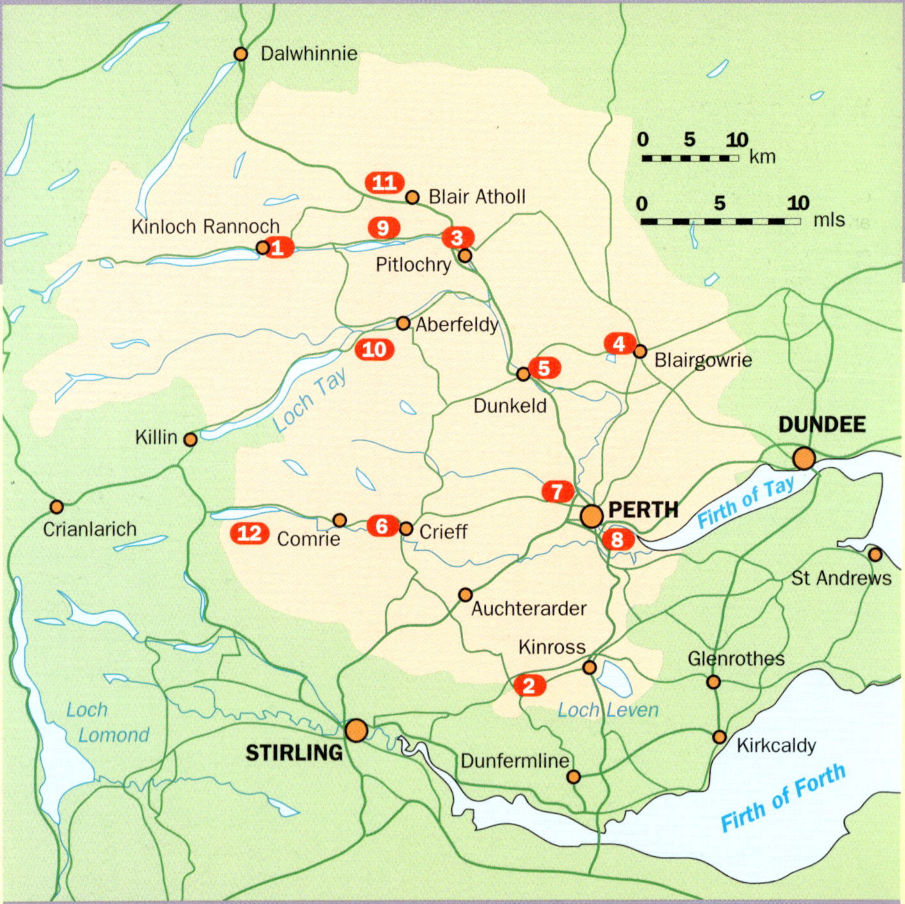

		Grade	Distance		Climb	page
1	Kinloch Rannoch circuit	■□□□□	3.2km	2 miles	50m (165ft)	6
2	Rumbling Bridge & R. Devon	■□□□□	5.6km	3.5 miles	40m (130ft)	8
3	Faskally Wood & Lochs	■□□□□	6.4km	4 miles	90m (300ft)	10
4	The Knockie & Ardblair	■■□□□	9.6km	6 miles	170m (560ft)	12
5	Dunkeld Trees & Lochs	■■□□□	11.2km	7 miles	150m (500ft)	14
6	Laggan Hill & Monument	■■□□□	10.4km	6.5 miles	215m (700ft)	18
7	Rivers Tay & Almond	■■□□□	18.4km	11.5 miles	70m (230ft)	20
8	Moncreiffe Hill & Forts	■■■□□	8.4km	5.25 miles	305m (1000ft)	22
9	Allean Forest & Stones	■■■□□	10.4km	6.5 miles	250m (820ft)	24
10	Aberfeldy to Kenmore	■■■□□	16.8km	10.5 miles	450m (1475ft)	26
11	Falls of Bruar & Creag Urrard	■■■■□	17.6km	11 miles	485m (1600ft)	28
12	Ben Vorlich & Stuc a' Chroin	■■■■■	15.2km	9.5 miles	1250m (4100ft)	30

Walk information

The walk grade reflects the amount of climbing involved, the quality of the paths and the nature of the terrain.

gentle
strenuous

In the walk descriptions, grid references are given (**in grey**) for the start point and for each numbered route point, as shown on the map of each walk. These can be used in conjunction with an Ordnance Survey map or as GPS waypoints.

The time given is an approximate indication of how long a walk will take, allowing some time to look at things of interest – you may go faster or slower. Several walks have options for shortcuts.

Safety in the hills

This guide includes a map of every route, but for walks in the higher hills and mountains (especially **Walk 12**), you are strongly advised to carry a compass and a full-sized map, which will show you more of the surrounding area and help with navigation if you stray from the route.

For those walks, you should carry adequate equipment for your comfort and safety: a full set of waterproofs, spare warm clothing, food and drink, torch and a whistle. In winter conditions, ice axe and crampons may be needed. Weather can change very rapidly at higher altitudes and the summits are usually colder and windier than the start point. It is also sensible to let someone know when and where you are going, and your expected return time.

Key to walk maps 1 – 12

ground above 1000m	**loch, reservoir**
ground 900m – 1000m	**river, stream**
ground 800m – 900m	**vehicle track, power line**
ground 700m – 800m	**motorway, A road, minor road**
ground 600m – 700m	**path, footbridge**
ground 500m – 600m	**railway (with station)**
ground 400m – 500m	**bus stop, toilets**
ground 300m – 400m	**notable tree, mast**
ground 200m – 300m	**car park, tourist information**
ground 100m – 200m	**garden, castle, church**
ground below 100m	**route, numbered waypoint**
woodland and forest	**summit (with / without trig)**
built up area	**crags, scree, earthwork**

6

Carriage drives and riverside paths enjoyed by the gentry in Georgian times are today a delightful way to explore the attractive scenery around Crieff.

Laggan Hill & Baird's Monument

Start Crieff – Macrosty Park car park **NN858221**

Grade ■■□□□

Distance 10.4km (6.5 miles)

Ascent 215m (700ft)

Time 3.5 hours

Terrain Paths and gently undulating tracks, over wooded hills and beside the River Earn.

Getting there: From West High Street in Crieff (the A85) follow Comrie Street then Milnab Street to the car park.

Public transport: Buses from Perth and elsewhere to Crieff.

The walk follows parts of the waymarked Crieff Path network. Along the way, look out for benches decorated with verses and various metal sculptures depicting heron, salmon and other aspects of local life.

MacRosty Park was opened in 1902 and later extended by the addition of Taylor and Mungall Parks. It contains an impressive collection of conifers, including noble fir, Douglas fir, Norway spruce and cedar of Lebanon. In 2010, a regeneration project set about giving it a new lease of life.

PERTHSHIRE BIG TREE COUNTRY

Eppie Callum's Tree is an ancient oak, believed to be 600 years old. It was supposedly grown from an acorn by Eppie Callum, the keeper of the Oakbank Inn, which stood on one of the cattle droving routes into Crieff.

Baird's Monument is a large granite obelisk erected in 1832, by his wife, to the memory of General Sir David Baird. During his distinguished military career, he won battles in India, Egypt, South Africa and Spain.

Lady Mary's Walk is named after Lady Mary Murray, who enjoyed strolling on the banks of the River Earn. She lived at Ochtertyre, a big house above Loch Monzievaird, from where carriage drives extended over Laggan Hill. Her father, Sir Patrick Murray, opened the walk to the people of Crieff in 1825.

ABOVE: *Wooded Laggan Hill from the south*

RIGHT: *Baird's Monument (Point 6)*

1 NN858221 From the car park, cross Turret Bridge and follow the road, past Eppie Callum's Tree, to 2. *An alternative route is through the park, following the Turret Burn upstream to a gate (that is on a right of way, but may be locked at night) then through chalets to the road.*

2 NN856226 Immediately beyond the entrance to Turretbank Drive, turn left up a grassy path through a strip of young trees. Enter a field by a kissing gate and head uphill. At the top, turn right along the hedgerow, passing under mature oak trees. Shortly before Currochs farm, go through a kissing gate in the hedge, walk a few paces towards the farm then turn left up a grassy track, which gradually climbs uphill with fine views to Crieff.

3 NN847224 Go through a gate into the woodland around disused Laggan Quarry, bear left to a T-junction and turn right. The track now meanders pleasantly over the crest of wooded Laggan Hill. Keep straight ahead where a path comes in from the left and follow the track as it bends right past Puddock Pond.

4 NN832224 Turn left at a T-junction 300m beyond the pond. Continue through woodland with open views through the overgrown beech hedge on the right. Pass a field on your left, where roe deer often graze, and keep ahead where another track joins from the right.

5 NN825220 Look out for a large boulder called Samson's Stone, where the panorama extends over Strathearn to Comrie. Beyond, the track bends left and narrows to a path. It goes downhill, veers right through a small, marshy valley then bends left to a T-junction. Turn left onto a path that spirals upwards around a craggy hill to Baird's Monument.

6 NN824217 The imposing granite obelisk, with inscriptions on four sides, rises from a thicket of bushes and trees. Return down the same path and keep straight ahead past the junction to descend to a road.

7 NN822215 Turn left by a cottage and in 20m turn left again onto a hard track past Trowan farm. Beyond the farm, the track runs between fields and becomes grassy. It rises slightly, giving open views, then descends through a tunnel of blackthorn. The way kinks left by an old gate and narrows to an earth path.

8 NN836218 As you enter woodland, a broad track lies ahead and you Immediately turn right for Lady Mary's Walk. Follow the path to the lively River Earn then walk downstream past mature beech, oak, larch and sweet chestnut trees.

9 NN852217 On reaching a cathedral-like beech avenue, fork right by a footpath sign onto a narrower, rougher path at the water's edge. As the Earn bends right, continue ahead to the Turret Burn on a path that goes uphill to bypass an eroded section of bank. Follow the burn to the road and turn right across Turret Bridge, back to the car park.

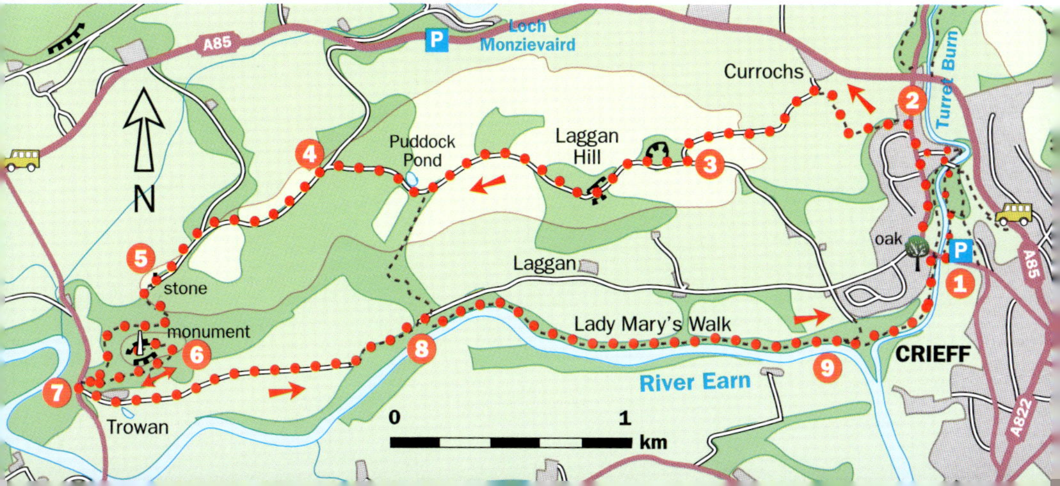

7

Firm, flat riverside paths lead from the centre of Perth through a patchwork of fields and woods to an attractive village where big oaks shade the green.

Rivers Tay & Almond

Start	Perth – River Tay viewpoint **NO121236**
Grade	■■□□□
Distance	up to 18.4km (11.5 mls)
Ascent	70m (230ft)
Time	5 hours
Terrain	Paths and tracks beside rivers and through fields; surfaces are tarmac or smooth gravel, except a rougher section near 6.

Getting there: The River Tay viewpoint is on Tay Street, at the east end of High Street. Pay & display car parks at Thimble Row (near 9) and Kinnoull Street.

Public transport: Bus and train services to Perth. Regular buses link Perth and Pitcairngreen.

Scone Palace can be seen across the River Tay on this walk. Its grounds include a spectacular pinetum with avenues of enormous conifers. The plant explorer David Douglas, who discovered many of Britain's important forest trees in North America, started his working life as an apprentice in the gardens.

North Inch is one of Perth's most popular open spaces for recreation, and contains sports fields and a golf course. The parkland is scattered with trees, in particular a fine line of tall limes on the southwest edge.

Perth Lade was constructed around 1150 and is Scotland's oldest canal. It used to provide Perth with its domestic water supply, as well as driving mills and serving as a defensive moat. It divides in two at the City Mills, and now runs under Mill Street and Canal Street to the Tay.

As the route is a figure of eight, with the paths crossing at Almond Bridge, you can do half the walk at a time: from Perth (**1** to **3** and **7** to **9**) or Pitcairngreen (**5** to **7** and **3** to **5**). Alternatively, break it into two linear walks using the bus to return to the start point. The path beside the Tay and Almond rivers is part of National Cycle Network route 77 and is marked with blue signs.

1 **NO121236** Walk up the River Tay from the viewpoint to the arched stone bridge, dating from 1771. Keep right to go under the bridge to the North Inch, then follow the tarmac riverside path. Cross the golf course, bearing away from the Tay, then go sharp right at a T-junction.

RIGHT: *Perth Bridge and artworks along the flood wall beside the River Tay (near Point 1)*

2 **NO115252** Go left through the flood wall and continue on the riverside path, ignoring all left turns. Scone Palace grounds can be seen across the water, until the Woody Islands obscure the view. Beyond them, the path bends left to run beside the River Almond.

3 **NO097266** The riverside path dips under a railway bridge, the A9 bridge and Almond Bridge, the old stone road bridge. Keep on the path, ignoring all left turns, all the way to Almondbank. Approach the village past a weir and sluice gate, the intake for Perth Lade.

4 **NO067258** At Almondbank, cross the river by a footbridge (signed NCN 77) then turn left up a lane to a junction on a bend. Walk ahead, uphill, on the main road and follow it to Pitcairngreen, which has an attractive village green.

5 **NO064269** Just before Pitcairngreen Inn (a possible lunch stop), turn right through Bridgeton Farm. Keep straight ahead on an unfenced track then grassy path between fields. The path enters weedy ground at the edge of Scots pine trees. Here cross a burn and go right alongside it on a rough field edge.

6 **NO070264** As soon as you enter the next field, turn left along its edge to a knoll of mature oak trees then walk to the right beside them. Pick up an earth track along the field edge, then join a broad, hard track running between fields and keep straight ahead for 2km to Berthapark. Go through the farmyard and on down the drive.

7 **NO094265** Beyond a cottage, keep right and cross Almond Bridge, which you went under earlier *(the riverside path is down to the left)*. Walk ahead through the industrial estate to a T-junction. Cross the road then go left to the Inveralmond Roundabout where a series of four pedestrian crossings take you onto the road into Perth.

8 **NO099258** Pass the next roundabout and then, immediately before a railway bridge over the road, turn right onto a path that runs between fences to the Perth Lade. Turn left beside the little canal, and follow it into the city centre. On the way, cross a footbridge over the railway and later the A85 Crieff Road (here go up steps, over a crossing and left to more steps, then go down these and keep ahead to return to the lade).

9 **NO113238** Beyond St Catherine's Retail Park, cross Caledonian Road by a pedestrian crossing. Where the lade runs under the City Mills (now a hotel) go left then first right through an arch. Turn right, past the hotel entrance, then left along Mill Wynd, which passes Perth Tourist Information Centre and bends right to the High Street. Turn left and keep straight ahead, across several junctions and through a pedestrian area, to the river.

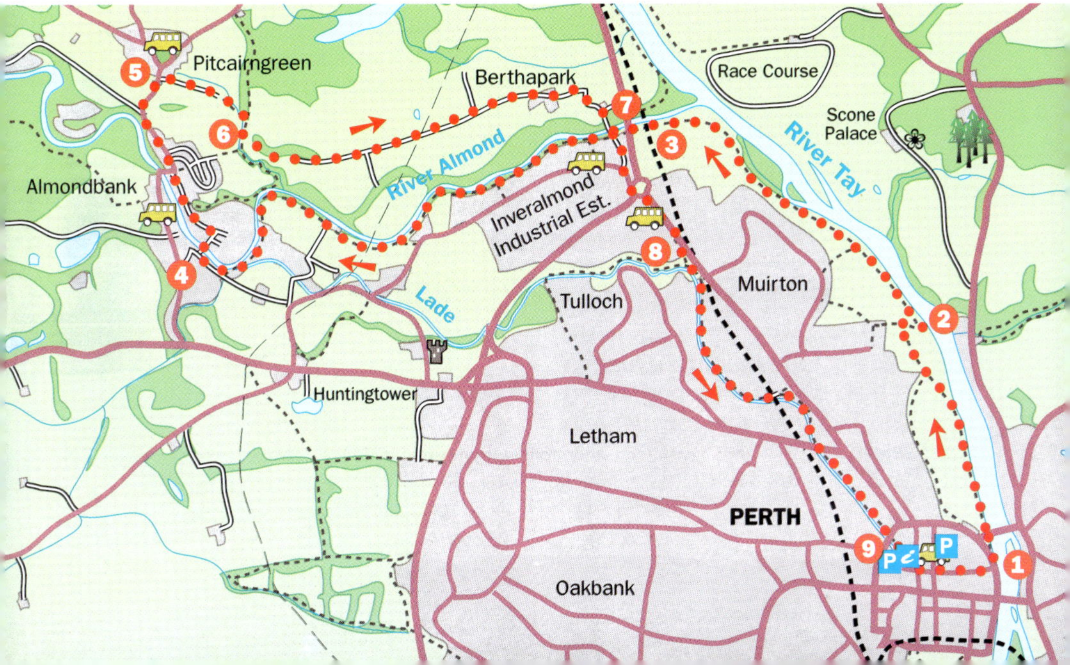

8

The two Iron Age hill forts on this walk are superb viewpoints, while tall trees, wooden sculptures and flitting butterflies provide interest within the wood.

Moncreiffe Hill & Forts

Start	near Perth – Woodland Trust car park on Rhynd road **NO138209**
Grade	■■□□□
Distance	8.4km (5.25 miles)
Ascent	305m (1000ft)
Time	3 hours
Terrain	Woodland paths around a steep-sided hill with wide views from two hillforts.

Getting there: Follow the A912 Edinburgh road out of Perth and turn left for Rhynd immediately before the M90 slip road; the car park is on the right after 1 mile.

Public transport: Take the Perth to Bridge of Earn bus up Edinburgh road, then walk 1km along Rhynd Road to Tarsappie and turn right up a track to **2**.

ABOVE: *Moncreiffe Hill from the south*

In 2010 the Woodland Trust acquired more land on the north side of Moncreiffe Hill and created a new car park and paths to make it more accessible to the residents of Perth. Geographically, the hill is very similar to Kinnoull Hill, which lies immediately to the north, across the Tay.

1 **NO138209** Head uphill on the track from the car park, enjoying ever wider views across the fields. The track zigzags uphill, through new tree plantings and past a wooden circle feature, then enters the bottom edge of the wood. Turn right at the first junction and walk along the hillside with conifers above and young deciduous trees below.

2 **NO131205** At a T-junction turn left (the track to the right comes in from the Rhynd road). Ignore the first left turn. Look out for a totem pole carved with local wildlife and a bench nearby with a view over Perth. Just beyond these, turn left at a broad junction onto a track that weaves uphill, passing more wooden sculptures. Pass below an open knoll and on its far side turn right onto a little path that angles back to its summit.

3 **NO131198** A trig point crowns the top of the knoll, which is the site of an Iron Age hill fort. The splendid view stretches over Bridge of Earn to the Ochil Hills, and beyond them to the conical peaks of East & West Lomond in Fife. Return to the track and continue along it. Fork right in 50m onto a track that climbs to the sunny, sheltered edge of the escarpment where butterflies are often seen. Turn right at a T-junction below the open, craggy hillock of Moredun Top.

Moncreiffe Hill is a wooded ridge lying between the Rivers Tay and Earn. It has a steep south-facing escarpment and dips more gently to the north. The name Moncreiffe derives from the Gaelic `Monadh Craiobh`, which means `hill of the tree'. The wood was bought in 1988 by the Woodland Trust, who have been working to make it more diverse and better for wildlife. It is home to red squirrels, roe deer, woodpeckers, buzzards, butterflies and many wildflowers. Tree species include Scots pine, Douglas fir, European larch, sycamore, birch, oak and ash.

Moredun Top is a large hillfort, enclosed by ruined walls, built during the Iron Age and enlarged during the Dark Ages. It is thought to have been the site of the 728AD battle between Angus and Alpin over control of the Pictish Kingdom. Look out for a socketed stone slab on the south side.

4 NO135198 Another 60m further on, turn right on to a path that goes diagonally downhill through larch trees. Halfway down, it passes through an old grove of Douglas firs. Turn left 50m before the bottom, above where the path meets a broad track by two more stately Douglas firs. Follow a narrow path that traverses the steep hillside. It gently rises then contours below crags and screes.

5 NO148195 At a T-junction, turn uphill on a track zigzagging to the top of the escarpment. At the top, continue left, back along the crest of the hill. Soon pass a bench with a splendid view to the south (a good picnic spot) and keep on until you are below Moredun Top. Just after passing **4** again, turn right up the slope then fork right onto a grassy path that spirals up onto the hillfort.

6 NO135199 From the cairn on the summit of Moredun Top there is a 360-degree view, which encompasses Kinnoull Hill and the Highlands to the north, as well as the Tay Estuary and Dundee in the east. Retrace your steps to the woodland and continue to the right. Turn right at a T-junction by an intriguing wood ant carving and walk downhill.

7 NO135202 At a junction, turn right onto a new path, which curves downhill past a giant slug sculpture. This brings you back to the track you started on. Turn right along it, soon leaving the mature wood and going downhill to the car park.

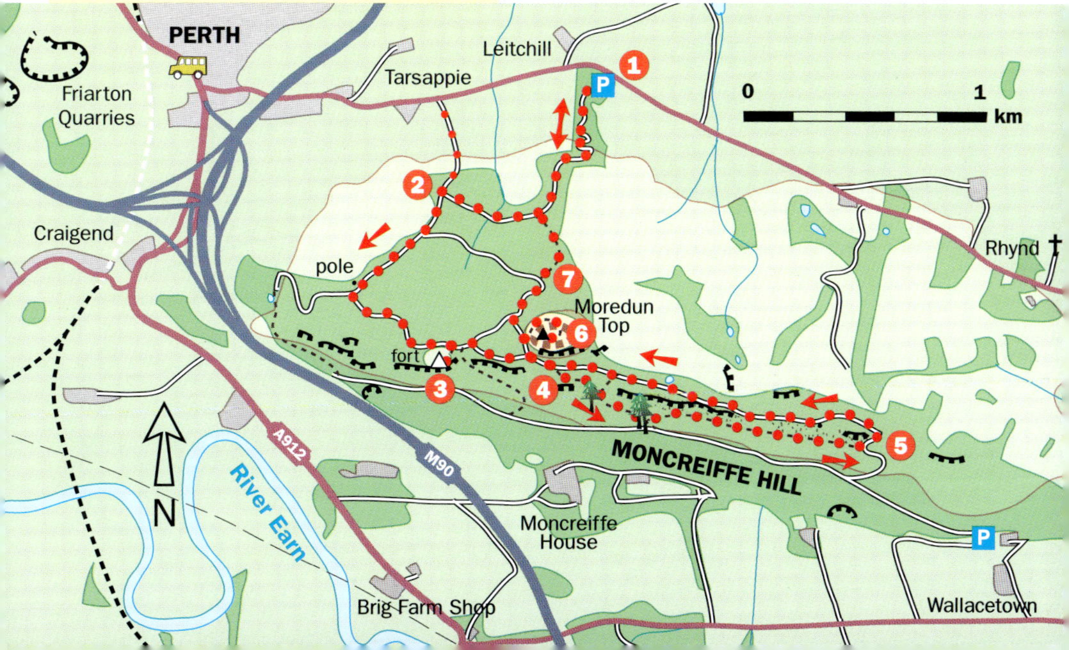

9

Trees grow fast and tall in Perthshire, as is evident in this south-facing Highland forest, which contains well preserved archaeological sites and lots of wildlife.

Allean Forest & Stones

Start	Loch Tummel – Allean Forest **NN858599**
Grade	■■■□□
Distance	10.4km (6.5 miles)
Ascent	250m (820ft)
Time	4 hours
Terrain	Paths and tracks climbing through an attractive conifer forest to open moorland with wide views.

Getting there: Allean Forest car park is on the B8019, 6.5 miles west of Pitlochry and 500m beyond Queen's View.

Public transport: Bus from Pitlochry to Queen's View Visitor Centre.

Two waymarked routes loop through the lower part of Allean Forest. This walk follows the red route, but leaves it to climb much higher to the stone circle. *The old track from **4** to **5** is rough and overgrown, especially in summer when bracken is thick. A less physical alternative is to stay on the forest road all the way past **7** to **5**.*

1 **NN858599** Take the path starting at the information board and pass to the right of the eco-toilets. Walk uphill under tall Norway spruce trees,

Allean Forest is a diverse forest with a wide mix of conifers. The most visited parts are being managed as continuous cover forestry, where regular thinning creates an open forest with tall trees. Other parts undergo a cycle of felling and replanting, resulting in a patchwork of different aged trees. Red squirrels, roe deer and pine marten live in the forest, and butterflies and wild flowers thrive in the more open areas.

Traces of human presence stretch back 4,000 years to a four poster stone circle, Na Clachan Aoraidh (the stones of worship). The walk also visits an 8th century Pictish ring fort and the Clachan, a partly restored 18th century farmstead.

Queen's View, the Forestry Commission visitor centre for Tay Forest Park, has displays and an audio-visual show about Big Tree Country, as well as a shop, café and picnic tables. Here you can admire one of Scotland's most photographed views. It was named after Queen Isabella, wife of Robert the Bruce, who ruled Scotland between 1306 and 1329, but it is often associated with Queen Victoria, who took tea here in 1866. Open 10am to 6pm from April to October.

ABOVE: *Looking towards Schiehallion from the viewpoint (Point 2)*

crossing a footbridge over a stream. At a forest road turn left, then go across a junction onto a path on the far side. This climbs under big Grand fir then through a light and airy larch wood to the Clachan.

2 NN853602 Keep left along the path from the Clachan information board, soon branching left to visit a viewpoint looking over Loch Tummel to Schiehallion. Returning to the path, continue uphill, crossing a footbridge.

3 NN851604 Cross a forest road onto a path that goes diagonally uphill to the right. Walk through an area that was clear felled a few years ago and is now full of young trees, both planted and naturally regenerated. The path bends left around a knoll of Scots pine and climbs to a forest road. Turn right along it.

4 NN856604 In 350m, the yellow route goes right. Look out in another 40m for a not very obvious old track that cuts back uphill to the left. Follow it through mature forest then across an area with young trees, where wild flowers and butterflies are prolific. It bends right at the top of this area to a junction. Go left and follow the track that soon runs along the right edge of a newly felled area.

5 NN851617 Emerge onto a forest road and turn left. Here, there is a superb view northwards over young trees to the Atholl mountains. Keep left at junction at the end of the replanted area to continue below an open hillside. Where the forest road bends left, keep straight ahead on a small path that climbs onto the open moorland.

6 NN838620 The stone circle is on your left at the top of the hillock, Meall nan Clachan. A great view stretches from Ben Vrackie in the east to Schiehallion in the southwest, with Farragon Hill due south. Return the same way to **5** then keep on along the forest road. Fork right at the next junction and rise up around the east side of Meall na h-Iolaire (hill of the eagle).

7 NN862604 About 500m beyond a hairpin bend, the forest road bends right by a wide junction. Go left off it onto a grassy path marked with a red-ringed post. After a pleasant descent through the forest turn right down a track.

8 NN863601 In 150m, turn left to visit the remains of the ring fort, a substantial stone-walled homestead. Return to the track and continue down it. Just before a junction with a forest road, turn left onto the outward path to return to the car park.

BELOW: *Allean Forest in autumn (Point 1)*

10

The panorama stretches over river, woods, loch and mountain on this high level linear walk that has a surprise in store at the Falls of Acharn.

Aberfeldy to Acharn & Kenmore

Start	Aberfeldy – the Square **NN856490**
Finish	Kenmore – car park **NN774453**
Grade	■■■□□
Distance	12 or 16.8km (7.5 or 10.5 miles)
Ascent	450m (1475ft)
Time	3.5 to 6 hours
Terrain	Tracks and paths contouring through woods and pasture high above Strath Tay.

Getting there: Leave the A9 at Ballinluig and drive 9 miles along the A827 to Aberfeldy. Kenmore is a further 6 miles west.

Public transport: Buses link Aberfeldy and Kenmore several days a week; check www.travelinescotland.com or phone 0871 200 22 33 for times.

At **Kenmore Hill**, Bolfracks Estate is conserving remains of an ancient pine wood. Replanting with Scots pines and other native species has restored the tree cover. Wildlife includes the rare black grouse.

PERTHSHIRE BIG TREE COUNTRY

At the **Falls of Acharn** a high waterfall cascades down a sheer rock. Hidden within a wooded gorge, it is best seen from the balcony of the Hermit's Cave.

The Scottish Crannog Centre features a unique reconstruction of an early Iron Age loch-dwelling. It is open daily from 1st April to 31st October, and on weekends throughout November.

Bolfracks garden is open to the public from 1 April to 31 October under Scotland's Gardens Scheme. Access is from the A827.

For a relaxed walk with no time pressure, leave your car in Kenmore and catch the bus to the start in Aberfeldy. Much of the route follows the Rob Roy Way, a long distance walk from Drymen to Pitlochry.

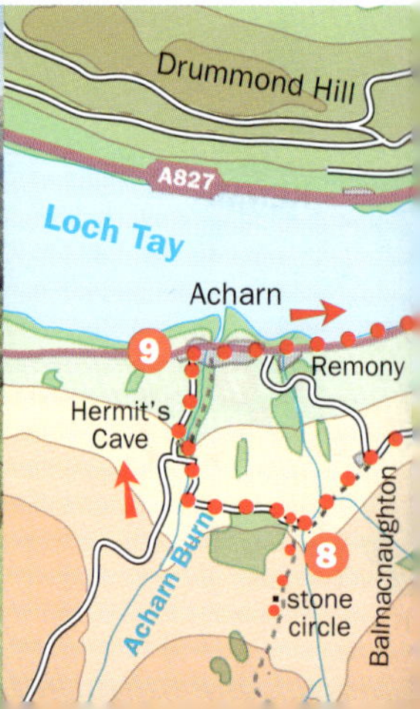

1 NN856490 From the Square in Aberfeldy walk 50m west along the A827, then turn left through the war memorial arch. Follow the path through the lower Birks of Aberfeldy, crossing footbridges over Moness Burn and a lade (millstream) serving the Watermill (now a bookshop and café). Climb steps to the A826 main road then, at a gap in the wall, cross over to Urlar Road and walk up it.

2 NN854482 Just before the drive to Urlar Farm, fork right onto a lane that contours above Aberfeldy with wide views over the River Tay to Weem and Castle Menzies. Keep left at Dunskaig, an old farm steading redeveloped as homes, then fork left and zigzag uphill on a gravel track. After 400m, pass to the left of a house and go through a gate onto a grassy track that continues climbing.

3 NN833477 Enter Bolfracks Wood and, after fording a little burn, keep left and head uphill. After passing under power lines, the track runs downhill to the end of the wood. Continue through open pasture, keeping to the main track and passing twice under another power line.

4 NN808472 At Tullichuil, which is screened by young trees, turn left through a gate into woodland (not ahead into a field). Follow a track that steadily climbs for 800m. Once you leave the wood, a superb view stretches to the right over the Tay to Schiehallion. Once past three old pine trees, you can see Loch Tay and Ben Lawers ahead. After entering another forest, the track bends right, downhill.

5 NN791455 The track by-passes a white tower house and soon leaves the forest. Where it goes through a gate, leave it and continue ahead across the grass with a wall on your right. Join another track and turn left up it. Beyond a shed, fork right and cross a burn.

6 NN789446 Meet a minor road at Tombuie Cottage. Turn right across the road bridge and walk 750m downhill, ignoring a turn to a woodland walks car park. *For the shorter option, stay on the road, which zigzags down to Kenmore.*

7 NN782447 For the full route, go left on a track and cross a ladder stile into the wood. Beyond an information board, follow the grassy path that contours along the hillside through young trees. Leave the wood by another ladder stile and keep ahead on a track across pasture. Pass to the left of Balmacnaughton and follow a grassy way across fields.

8 NN766431 Cross a footbridge over Remony Burn. *A detour 600m uphill leads to a stone circle with a wall through its middle.* Continue along the contouring track, passing below a wood then curving downhill. Immediately before a bridge, turn right onto a path beside Acharn Burn. Go down two flights of steps, then turn left over a footbridge where the water cascades over sculpted rocks. Climb back up to the track and go right, downhill. Look out for the Hermit's Cave on your right. Follow the passageway, which has a step down, and turn right inside to a balcony where the Falls of Acharn are suddenly revealed. After leaving the cave, continue down the track to Acharn.

9 NN755438 Turn right and cross a road bridge into the pretty village of Acharn. Walk 2.5km along the road, passing the Scottish Crannog Centre. At the A827 junction, turn left into Kenmore village.

LEFT: *View across Loch Tay to Kenmore and Drummond Hill (from between Points 7 & 8)*

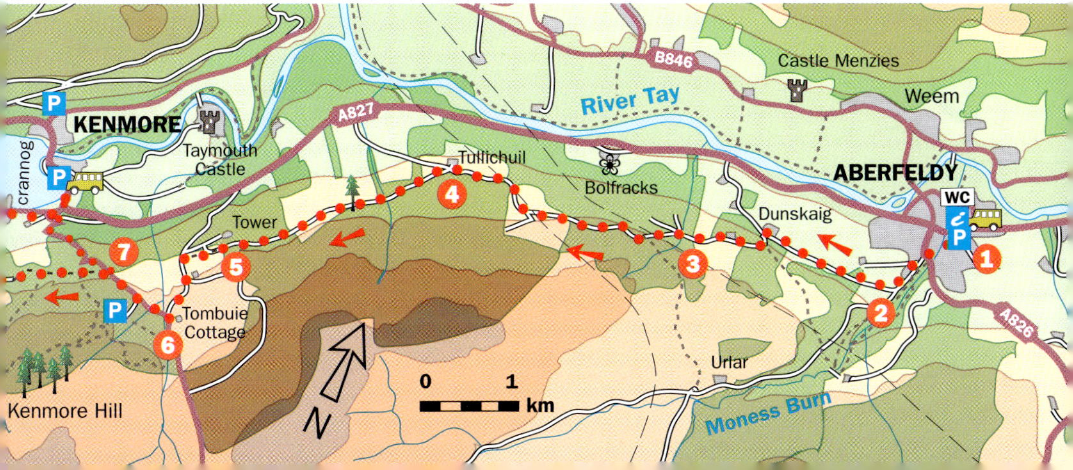

11

This walk in Cairngorms National Park goes from dramatic waterfalls and lofty trees to an ancient watch tower with a stunning view over mountain and glen.

Falls of Bruar & Creag Urrard

Start Bruar – House of Bruar car park **NN821659**

Grade ■□□□□

Distance 12 or 17.6km (7.5 or 11 miles)

Ascent 485m (1600ft)

Time 5 or 7 hours

Terrain Paths by a wooded gorge, then forest tracks to a heathery hilltop with mountain views.

Getting there: Leave the A9 at Bruar, 40 miles north of Perth, and follow signs into the House of Bruar.

Public transport: Bus service from Pitlochry, via Blair Atholl.

This walk starts from House of Bruar, famed for its quality country clothing, restaurant and food hall. It climbs to an ancient watch tower on Creag Urrard for a magnificent view over Highland Perthshire. Keep dogs under close control to avoid disturbing the rich and varied wildlife, which includes black grouse and other ground nesting birds.

ABOVE: *View from the watch tower (Point 5)*

OPPOSITE: *The Lower Bridge at the Falls of Bruar*

1 NN821659 Go through a gap in the buildings to Bruar Water, a fast flowing burn. Turn left up the path and go though an archway under a railway line. Walk through Scots pine woodland to the Lower Bridge and Falls, where the river tumbles under a natural rock arch. Cross the bridge and continue uphill on the path. At a bench by a wide bend in a forest road, pause for a view of the Upper Falls, then follow the upper arm of the forest road.

The Falls of Bruar have been a popular beauty spot for over 200 years. In 1787 Robert Burns visited the steep gorge of the Bruar Water, which was then devoid of woodland. He wrote a poem pleading with his host, the 4th Duke of Atholl, to "shade my banks wi' towering trees, and bonnie spreading bushes". A few years after Burns' death, his wishes were granted when the duke planted Scots pine and European larches on the rocky banks. He also built the paths and bridges that are still in use today.

Perthshire BIG TREE COUNTRY

Baluain Wood is one of Scotland's finest larch woods, managed by Atholl Estates to produce tall, straight stemmed trees whose timber is a valuable building material. Red squirrels and roe deer thrive in this habitat.

2 **NN825665** After going 500m through larch woodland, a well-used forest road joins from the left (the return route). Keep straight ahead, walking on the level way for 2km through Baluain Wood.

3 **NN846663** Shortly after passing through a stone wall with a deer fence on top, fork left onto a lesser track (marked with a blue arrow), where the forest road bends downhill. Steadily climb through the wood until the track bends left and levels off.

4 **NN856673** At a wide junction by an open area, just before the track up Glen Banvie, turn left uphill. Fork right after 300m and climb through mature woodland to heather moorland with scattered, open-grown pines. The view to the left over a felled area stretches across Glen Garry to Farragon Hill and Schiehallion. At the high point of the track, immediately before a wall, turn right on a rough way through the heather.

5 **NN845672** Climb past a shelter cairn to the ruined stone watch tower atop Creag Urrard (443m/1453ft), where there is a splendid view south to Blair Castle and Ben Vrackie, and north into the Cairngorms. Beinn Dearg and the Beinn a' Ghlo range look massive and very close. Return to the track and go left back to **4**, then keep left at the next two junctions. *For the shorter option, go right down the track to* ***8****.*

6 **NN853677** Leave the forest by a deer gate and walk 3km up Glen Banvie, with a view over Banvie Burn to open moorland. The plantation on the left is enclosed by a deer fence that has battens to make it more visible to low-flying grouse. Look out for the ruined walls of an abandoned farming settlement below a cairn-topped hill.

7 **NN826697** Where the track crests the rise, ignore the turn to the right (up Glen Bruar) and stay on the main track, soon curving downhill to the left. Walk through open Scots pine woodland then cross a stile into denser woodland. For the next 1.5 miles (2.4km), dogs should be kept on a lead during the bird breeding season (April–July).

8 **NN823670** At a track junction, keep ahead and descend more steeply to **2**. Turn right to return to the bench overlooking the gorge and go right, uphill, on the path to the Upper Bridge. Cross the bridge above the Upper Falls and return down the far side, where the path is rougher. Continue past the Lower Bridge, retracing your steps to House of Bruar.

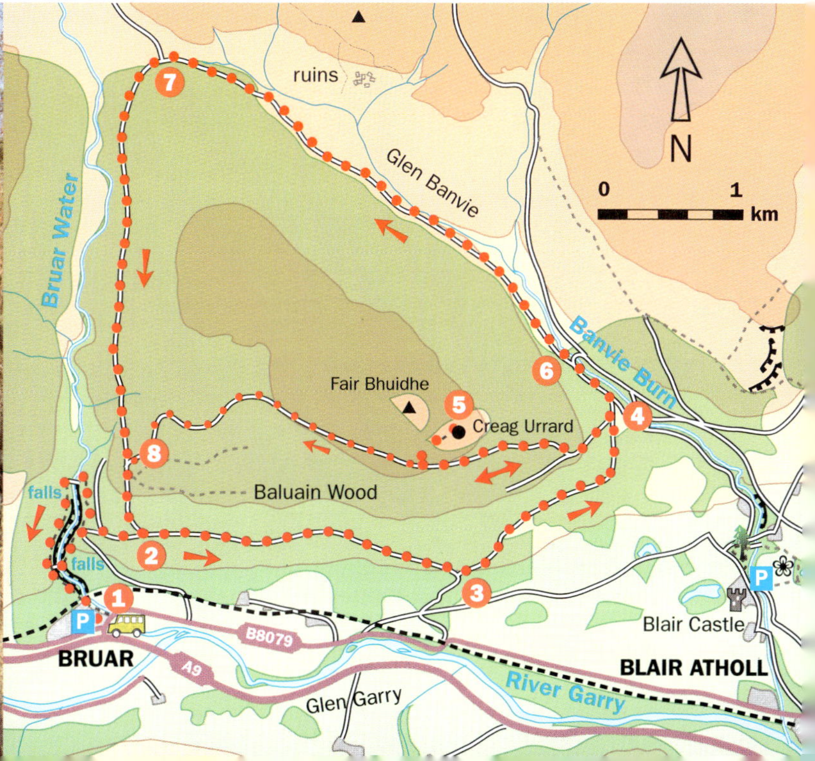

12

A pair of Munros rise above pretty Ardvorlich on the shore of Loch Earn – the first is a popular and straightforward climb, the second requires more nerve and agility.

Ben Vorlich & Stuc a' Chroin

Start	Loch Earn – Ardvorlich **NN633232**
Grade	☐☐☐☐☐
Distance	10 or 15.2km (6 or 9.5 miles)
Ascent:	885m or 1250m (2900ft or 4100ft)
Time:	4 to 8 hours
Terrain:	Good mountain path up Ben Vorlich, steep and stony near the summit; tougher going over Stuc a' Chroin, with some easy rock scrambling.

Getting there: Drive 12 miles west from Crieff on the A85 to St Fillans, then follow the South Loch Earn road 4.5 miles to Ardvorlich; park in the pull-in west of the stone bridge.

Public transport: None available.

ABOVE: *Starting the climb up Stuc a' Chroin, with Ben Vorlich behind (after Point 6)*

These Munros (mountains over 3,000ft/914m) lie within Loch Lomond and The Trossachs National Park. Sheep farming and deer stalking are the main activities of the local estate, so it's important to keep dogs under close control.

1 NN633232 Walk through the urn-topped pillars on the east side of the bridge and along an avenue of limes and other trees. Fork right to cross a bridge over Ardvorlich Burn and immediately turn left up a small track. Walk uphill, beside the steep, wooded burn valley. Go through a succession of fences, by gate or stile, as you climb through sheep pasture then alder woodland. Trees around the burn are protected by a deer fence to allow regeneration.

2 NN630218 Go right at a fork, staying on the track and climbing away from the fence (the grassy path on the left is the through route to Callendar and Glen Artney). Cross a bridge over one side stream then ford a smaller one.

3 NN630211 Just above a new hydro-electric dam, cross a bridge over the burn flowing out of Coire Bhuide, the wide bowl of moorland on the north side of Ben Vorlich. The track ends here and you continue through the heather on a well-made path, heading up the right side of the north ridge of Ben Vorlich.

4 NN629198 Beyond a flight of stone steps, the path climbs onto the crest of the ridge. Climb to the summit cone, where a steep stony path zigzags up to the trig point at the top of Ben Vorlich (985m/3232ft). It is worth going 150m east along the summit ridge to a cairn for the full view. Ben Lawers lies to the north and nearby Meall na Fearna due east.

5 NN629189 *To miss out Stuc a' Chroin, return northwards by the way you came.* For the full route, descend westwards on a rough path that stays close to a sheer drop on the left and soon bends southwest. Descend steeply past crags to a peaty dip and continue to the lowest point between the two mountains.

6 NN621183 Beyond the bealach (pass), the path climbs the right side of the ridge ahead then bends left on the edge of a boulderfield to the crest. At the foot of the daunting rock face, go diagonally right across the boulders, then up a path under the main rock face. It zigzags steeply upwards and includes a short scramble up a rock crack. Pass a cairn on the north top and cross two dips to the summit cairn.

7 NN617174 From Stuc a' Chroin (975m/3198ft), you look across Dubh Choirein (the black corrie) to the steep south face of Ben Vorlich. In the west, Stob Binnein and Ben More rise beyond Loch Voil. To descend, retrace your steps to the nearer dip, fork left to a small cairn on the northwest ridge, then go down the ridge 200m.

8 NN615180 Turn right at a larger cairn, onto a path that zigzags very steeply down into grassy Coire Fhuadaraich – take care as it is easy to slip. Cross a stream and contour around the corrie, over boggy and rocky ground before rising up onto Ben Vorlich's northwest ridge.

9 NN621193 The path bends right as it crosses the ridge and then curves around Coire Buidhe to the north ridge. It rejoins the outward path about 100m above the flight of stone steps (at **4**). Turn left down the path to return to Ardvorlich.

Ben Vorlich is one of Perthshire's most distinctive mountains, with a conical summit visible from much of Strathearn and the Forth valley. The path up it was very boggy in places, until Perth and Kinross Countryside Trust funded remedial work that greatly improved the walking.

Neighbouring **Stuc a' Chroin** looks more like a sphinx from a distance. The 'face' is a rock buttress, up which a steep path winds, giving an exhilarating climb requiring the use of hands as well as feet.

Ardvorlich has been the home of the Stewarts of Ardvorlich since 1580. Sir Walter Scott fictionalised the exploits of the clan in his novel The Legend of Montrose. A gravestone by the bridge commemorates seven MacDonalds from Glencoe who raided Ardvorlich in 1620 and were killed when the Stewarts returned unexpectedly.

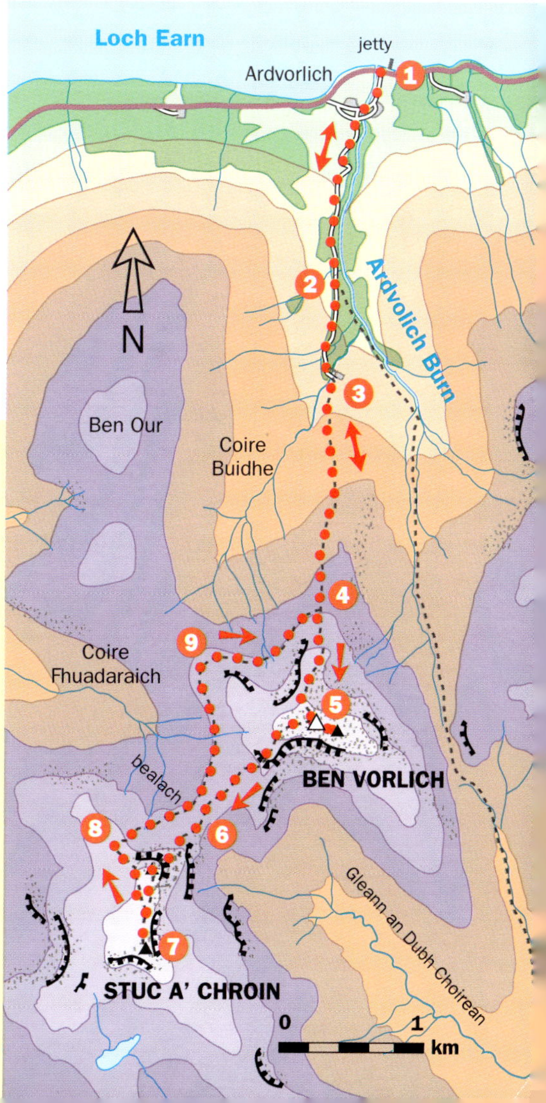

Enjoying the outdoors

Perth and Kinross Council have a duty to uphold public access rights and you should contact their access officers if you find any route obstructed. The council employs countryside rangers, who help people to enjoy the outdoors responsibly and who organise events such as guided wildlife walks.

Several other organisations also promote access on their land–often with waymarked paths–and employ rangers who assist the public and carry out nature conservation work.

A Perthshire Big Tree Country guide to *Countryside Events and Guided Walks* is published each year, listing outdoor events being organised by these various organisations. There is also a *Perthshire Big Tree Country* guide to dozens of places you can visit to enjoy the area's unique woodland heritage and magnificent landscape. These free guides can be picked up at visitor information centres.

Perth and Kinross Council
Community Greeenspace
01738 475349
www.pkc.gov.uk

Forestry Commission Scotland
Tay Forest Park
01350 728641
www.forestry.gov.uk

Scottish Natural Heritage
01738 444177
www.snh.gov.uk

The National Trust for Scotland
01350 728641
www.nts.org.uk

Scottish Wildlife Trust
Loch of the Lowes
01350 727337
www.swt.org.uk

Atholl Estates
01796 481646 or 481355
www.athollestatesrangerservice.co.uk

Enjoy Scotland's outdoors responsibly

SCOTTISH OUTDOOR ACCESS CODE

KNOW THE CODE BEFORE YOU GO
outdooraccess-scotland.com

Everyone has the right to be on most land and inland water providing they act responsibly. Your access rights and responsibilities are explained fully in the Scottish Outdoor Access Code.

Whether you're in the outdoors or managing the outdoors, the key things are to:

- **take responsibility for your own actions**
- **respect the interests of other people**
- **care for the environment.**

Visit **outdooraccess-scotland.com** or contact your local Scottish Natural Heritage office.